The Mirabal Sisters
From Caterpillars to Butterflies

The Mirabal Sisters
From Caterpillars to Butterflies

Text by **Raynelda A. Calderón**
Illustrations by **María Ocampo**

Cayena Press, Inc.
New York

Long ago, the Dominican Republic was **ruled** by a president who allowed people very little freedom. Under this **dictatorship**, four beautiful little sisters lived with their parents in a small town called Ojo de Agua. Their names? Patria, Dedé, Minerva, and María Teresa Mirabal.

The girls received so much love from their parents! They grew up surrounded by many family members—uncles, aunts, cousins—and had many friends with whom they played dolls and *mata-rile-rile-ron.* They went to the nearby river to play and bathe, walked in the mountains, rode horses, and freely ran up and down the streets. They were very happy!

At night, Patria, Dedé, Minerva, and María Teresa loved to sit down to listen to the stories and tales that the adults in the house would tell. They especially liked the stories of flying witches, the stories of the Bible, and the stories of **Juan Bobo** and **Pedro Animal.**

In addition to learning to read and write in elementary school, they learned embroidery and how to be *una buena ama de casa* (a good mother and respectful wife) as it was **customary** to teach in those days. By fifth grade, their parents sent them to study at a nuns' school to finish their high school education.

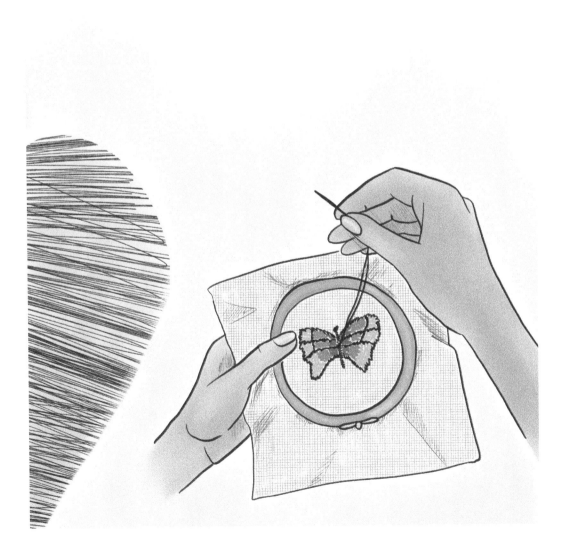

The sisters grew up very close and attached to each other; they loved each other intensely and told each other everything. When they grew up, they liked to visit other towns nearby to meet new people, go to parties, and dance *¡hasta que los pies les dolieran!*

Patria, the oldest, liked to paint and draw flowers. She was always in a good mood, with a smile on her lips. She enjoyed helping others, but most of all, she loved pampering and pleasing her sisters. She was always well-groomed, and she liked to do interior decoration. Her favorite season was Christmas—because she could hang all types of Christmas arrangements around the house. She dreamed of visiting Havana, Cuba!

Dedé, the second sister, liked to make new friends. After school, she would go to her dad's store to help with his business. She was very good with math! She was in charge of the bills and keeping track of what was sold—rice, sugar, coffee, cotton fabrics—and even filled out basic medical prescriptions.

Minerva, the third born, was a **voracious** reader; she would read anything she could get a hold of. She loved flowers, animals, and poetry. She liked to work in the garden, which she kept very beautiful. In the afternoons, after her father had closed the store, they all used to sit *en la galeria*—in front of the house—to listen to Minerva **recite** the poems of famous poets like Pablo Neruda and Adolfo Becker.

She was also very interested in the country's **government affairs.** She dreamed of a free Dominican Republic, without the dictatorship of President Trujillo.

Everybody pampered María Teresa because she was the youngest sister—the baby of the family. She was kind and very curious. She would ask about everything! She had a good memory and wanted to study engineering. She also liked to cook, and, following in the footsteps of her sister Minerva, loved to read. Her hair was very long because she wouldn't trim it, and she liked to style it in a braid or two.

As time passed, the four sisters grew up and turned into loving and beautiful women. Patria, Dedé, Minerva, and María Teresa were different from other girls because they thought outside of the box. They liked being independent and did not follow the norms established for women at that time.

They wore pants and went to college, and Minerva was the
first woman in the area to drive a car.

Eventually, they met handsome boys with whom they
fell in love, got married, and had children.

Although they lived happily with their husbands and children, the cloud of the president's **dictatorship** was always hanging over them. You never knew what that man would do next through his **caliés!** As the president's **abuses** grew, citizens—especially the youth—began to form underground revolutionary groups or movements against him.

One of the most influential groups was the June 14 Movement, organized by Minerva. Naturally, her sisters and their husbands supported her cause.

The *June 14 Movement* became popular, and young people from all over the country joined against President Trujillo. Despite the group operating with great care, the President learned of the movement's existence and ordered the arrest of all those who were associated with it. He was especially furious that a woman, Minerva, dared to challenge him.

Because of Trujillo's threat, many people were afraid of being pointed out as *antitrujillista*—against Trujillo—and being put in jail. Therefore, people would call Minerva "the butterfly," a **code name.** When she arrived at a place, they would say "The butterfly is here."

Nonetheless, the Mirabal sisters and their husbands went to jail—**except** Dedé, who did not join the *June 14 Movement*, although she supported her sisters.

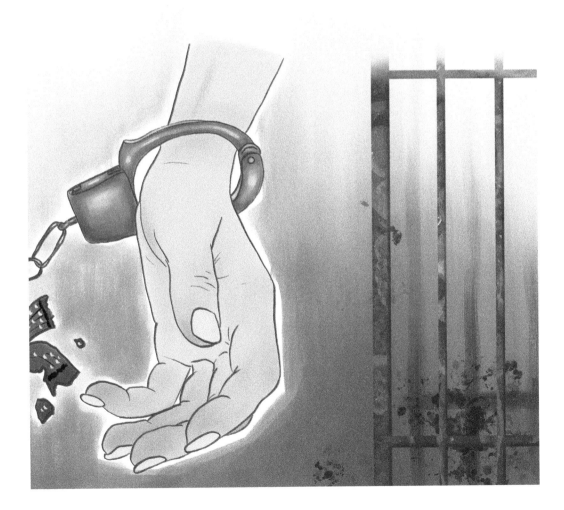

While her sisters were in jail, Dedé was in charge of taking care of all the children—hers and her sisters—along with her mother, *doña* Chea. She arranged for food and clothing to be delivered to them in jail. Dedé and her mother also **advocated** for their freedom.

After several months, the sisters were finally allowed to go home! However, they were under **house arrest**, so they couldn't go anywhere.

Because their husbands were not released, the sisters got a special permit to visit them in jail. Trujillo, the **tyrant**, took advantage of these trips to **ambush** the sisters and get rid of them.

On the afternoon of November 25, 1960, Patria, Minerva, and María Teresa were returning from one of these visits when *sicarios*—government assassins—killed the sisters and their driver, Rufino. Their bodies were left lying in the bushes.

At home, Dedé and her mother were very worried because it was already dark and the three women had not returned from their trip. The children were crying because they missed their mothers.

The next day, neighbors brought them the news that they had found the **lifeless** bodies of Patria, Minerva, María Teresa, and their driver, Rufino. The news turned the house upside down. Dedé and her mother were desperate. How had Trujillo dared to kill defenseless women?

25

The citizens were hurt by the death of the sisters and at the same time **outraged** by such a crime. Now, when talking about the girls, people called them *Las Mariposas*—The Butterflies. Someone reproduced a photo of the three sisters together, and that photo became popular.

Everybody wanted to have a photo of *Las Mariposas*! The memory of the sisters turned into a current of air that, with each flap, **propelled** the idea of a free Dominican Republic to the entire country.

The horror of the crime made world news, and the death of the sisters gave further **impetus** to the *June 14 Movement* that Minerva had started.

Just six months after the sisters' death, brave men **executed** Trujillo. Just like Minverva had **yearned for**, the Dominican Republic was free of dictatorship! *Las Mariposas* became a **symbol** of the fight for freedom.

Today, there are schools, streets, cities, poems, and postage stamps named after the Mirabal sisters. In their honor, the **United Nations** named November 25, the day of their murder, the **International Day for the Elimination of Violence Against Women** which is celebrated worldwide.

In their hometown, Dedé, the sister who survived to take care of her sisters' children and tell their story, made the house where they lived into a museum to honor the memory of Patria, Minerva, and María Teresa.

There are paintings, dresses, books, letters, … everything that the sisters left behind. The beautiful garden that Minerva cared for is also well kept. And, **amid** the flowers, you can see butterflies playing around. The Mirabal sisters.

Glossary

Advocate: A person who publicly supports or recommends a particular cause or policy. A person who pleads on someone else's behalf.

Ambush: A surprise attack by people lying in wait in a concealed position. Make a surprise attack on (someone) from a concealed position.

Amid: Surrounded by; in the middle of.

Antitrujillista: A person who used to oppose Trujillo or did not agree with his ruling.

Assassin: A murderer of an important person in a surprise attack for political or religious reasons.

Assassination: To murder (usually prominent person) by sudden or secret attack often for political reasons.

Caliés: The "calié" was an agent, a spy paid with State funds, who was part of an organized structure directed from the highest levels of the government's intelligence services, with surveillance, police, torture, and government functions.

Cause: A principle, aim, or movement that, because of a deep commitment, one is prepared to defend or advocate.

Code name: A word used for secrecy or convenience instead of the usual name.

Customary: According to the customs or usual practices associated with a particular society, place, or set of circumstances.

Dictator: A ruler with total power over a country, typically one who has obtained control by force.

Dictatorship: A country governed by a dictator.

Doña: Lady; Madam; a Spanish title of respect, used with the given name.

Except: Not included.

Execute: Kill (someone) as a political act.

Galería: A terrace; usually paved outdoor area adjoining a residence. Part of a house intended for moments of rest.

En la galería: In the terrace.

Government affairs: The exercise of political authority over the actions, affairs, etc., of a political unit, people, etc., as well as the performance of certain functions for this unit or body; the action of governing; political rule and administration.

Hasta que les dolieran los pies: ("until their feet ache") - Expression to indicate dancing so much that your feet ache.

House arrest: Court-ordered confinement in one's own home.

Impetus: The force that makes something happen or happen more quickly.

International Day for the Elimination of Violence Against Women: Women's rights activists have observed 25 November as a day against gender-based violence since 1981. This date was selected to honor the Mirabal sisters, three political activists from the Dominican Republic who were brutally murdered in 1960 by order of the country's ruler, Rafael Trujillo (1930-1961). In 2000, the United Nations designated November 25 as the International Day for the Elimination of Violence Against Women. It is an occasion for governments, international organizations and non-governmental organizations to raise public awareness of violence against women.

Juan Bobo: Folkloric character from Puerto Rico and the Dominican Republic for which children's books, songs, riddles and folktales have developed around him.

Lifeless: Dead or apparently dead. Lacking vigor, vitality, or excitement.

Maltreatment: Cruel or violent treatment of a person or animal; mistreatment.

Mata-rile-rile-ron: Puerto Rican play game; the game is played by two lines of children singing the stanzas alternately, or, at times, by a single girl and two lines of children that take turns alternating their stanzas with the solo stanzas of the girl. At the e nd, all join hands and dance in a circle.

Outrage: Arouse fierce anger, shock, or indignation in (someone).

Pedro Animal: Folkloric character from Puerto Rico and the Dominican Republic for which folktales have developed around him.

Propelled: drive, push, or cause to move in a particular direction, typically forward.

Recite: Repeat aloud or declaim (a poem or passage) from memory before an audience.

Revolutionary: Engaged in or promoting political revolution; involving or causing a complete or dramatic change.

Revolutionary movement: A social movement that seeks to bring about major changes in a society.

Rule: Exercise ultimate power or authority over (an area and its people)

Sicarios: In Spanish, it means a hired gunman or assassin.

Surround: Be all around (someone or something).

Symbol: A thing (or a person) that represents or stands for something else.

To think outside of the box: To explore ideas that are creative and unusual and that are not limited or controlled by rules or tradition.

Trujillo: A dictator who ruled the Dominican Republic for more than 30 years, assumed near-absolute control of the Caribbean nation in 1930. Full name: Rafael Leonidas Trujillo Molina.

Tyrant: A cruel and oppressive ruler; a person exercising power or control in a cruel, unreasonable, or arbitrary way.
Una buena ama de casa: It means being a good housewife or homemaker (keeping the house clean, the kids fed and entertained, making well-rounded meals, and maintaining a relationship with your spouse).

Underground: In or into secrecy or hiding, especially because of carrying out subversive political activities.

United Nations: Intergovernmental organization that aims to maintain international peace and security, develop friendly relations among nations, achieve international cooperation, and be a center for harmonizing the actions of nations.

Voracious: Having a very eager approach to an activity

Yearn: Have an intense feeling of longing for something, typically something that one has lost or been separated from.

Author's Note

From 1930 to 1961, the Dominican Republic was under the dictatorship of Rafael Leonidas Trujillo. Although I was born long after those years of tyranny, what my parents and grandparents told me, and what I have read about that time, filled me with curiosity and interest in knowing more about these events.

It is not known for sure what incited Trujillo's hatred against the Mirabal family. Some say that it was Minerva's defiance and dissent to Trujillo at a party; it could also have been that the family (at that same party) left the party before Trujillo, which was not allowed.

What is true is that from that night on, life changed for the Mirabal family. Not only were they arrested several times, but people stopped shopping at the store of don Enrique, the father of the sisters, out of fear. The business went bankrupt, and they had to shut it down. Government officials took possession of various lands, and properties were destroyed. In short, people say that during that time, it was better to be an enemy of the devil and not of Trujillo.

I grew up hearing about the Mirabal sisters that Trujillo had ordered to be killed, but I had never actually read anything (a book, a newspaper article) about them. I only knew what people would share. However, technology has made information about the Mirabals more accessible. Thinking that, as a child, I would have liked to read a book about them, I dared to write one.

This book is an independent study. The Mirabal family has not been consulted or involved in its preparation. In 2009,

Dedé Mirabal published her memoirs, "Vivas en su jardin," (Vintage Spanish). I referred to these memoirs and other reference works, magazines, and newspaper articles for information on the Mirabals for this picture book.

When talking about the Mirabal sisters, only Patria, Minerva, and María Teresa—the sisters who lost their lives at the hands of assassins sent by Trujillo on November 25, 1960—are mentioned. However, the Mirabals were four sisters. In this book I also include Dedé because she is the sister who was left alive to tell us the story—the fourth butterfly.

Raynelda

Illustration Process

I created the illustrations for this story in several stages. First, I read the story, and from the text, the basic ideas for each illustration spread were born.

The first sketches, or the storyboard, were fleeting and playful scratches that helped visualize the composition of the scene. I made annotations about details to add to the scenes, which helped me know what references I would need to consult when drawing.

In the next step, I visually documented information about the sisters. I did extensive research and created a bank of images for references; I tried to be as precise as possible regarding the time the sisters lived in.

Next came the creation of the files. I made a second sketch in which I used raw unfinished lines, and created the general composition of each page. I often needed visual references for the human figures. Sometimes I found free guides on the internet, and other times I had to take pictures of myself to help me figure it out (this step is always part of the process).

After this second sketch, I made the compositional corrections I saw necessary and, finally, started sketching clean lines—line art. The final touch of this stage was adding shading details on the clothes and characters, as well as small drawing corrections.

The next stage in the process was to create the color palette I would use to give life to the drawings, as well as the color palette for some pages that required a different atmosphere or finish.

The program I use to illustrate is *Procreate*, and I chose the brushes based on the style of the illustrations. I usually use three basic brushes (one for lines, one for applying color and shadows, and a third one for blending). I then use other brushes to add specific finishing touches. Depending on the complexity, this final stage can take from two to four hours for each illustration.

The result is this wonderful book, an incredible story and a process full of love and dedication.

Maria J.

About the Author

Raynelda grew up in the Dominican Republic on a healthy diet of romance novels, comic strips, Gabriel Garcia Marquez's books, and other literature. She spends her free time thinking about (and drafting) books to write.

As a librarian, working with children inspires her to create picture books that highlight the accomplishments of Hispanic women in history. Raynelda is the author of "Mama Tingo," "María Montez, the Queen of Technicolor," and "Little Giants: 10 Hispanic Women Who Made History."

"The Mirabal Sisters, From Caterpillars to Butterflies" is her fourth children's book.

Visit and Follow Raynelda at
www.rayneldacalderon.com
@raycc10

About the Illustrator

María is a passionate graphic designer. She grew up between Colombia and Spain. Her extreme curiosity has led her to live in 4 different countries, an experience that has enriched her life as well as her creative process, and has made her an eternal learner.

Check out her website at mographic-design.webflow.io

follow Maria @du.al_

Selected Bibliography

Alberto, E. G. (n.d.). Expedición y Movimiento 14 de Junio (República Dominicana). Retreived from https://www.monografias.com/trabajos48/expedicion-junio/expedicion-junio.shtml.

Behar, R. (May 1995). Revolutions of the Heart. Women's Review of Books, 12(8), 6-7.

Haag, J. (2002). "Mirabal Sisters." Women in World History: A biographical encyclopedia, edited by Anne Commire, vol. 11, Yorkin Publications, pp. 158-161. Gale Books.

Hanrahan, M. (2005, Fall). Remembering the Butterflies. Herizons, 19(2), 12.

Martin, J. (September 9, 2020). Trujillo, dictador a golpe de machete. La Vanguardia. Retrieved from https://www.lavanguardia.com/historiayvida/historia-contemporanea/20200816/27251/trujillo-dictador-golpe-machete.html

Mena, J. (March 1995). Women on the Verge… Four Brash Latina Writers Transform the Literary Landscape. Hispanic Magazine, 8(2), 22-24, 26.

Mujica, B. (April 1995). The Sisters Mirabal. The World & I, 10(4), 328-333.
Nieto, L. N., & Rubinstein, I. F. (2020). The Power of the Butterflies: The legacy of the Mirabal Sisters in an exhibition by the Mexican cartoonist Cintia Bolio. Feminist Encounters: A Journal of Critical Studies in Culture and Politics, 4(1), 03. Https://doi.org/10.20897/femenc/9707

Pruitt, S. (March 8, 2021). How the Mirabal Sisters Helped Topple a Dictator. Retrieved from https://www.history.com/news/mirabal-sisters-trujillo-dictator

Rohter, L. (February 15, 1997). Santo Domingo Journal: The Three Sisters, Avenged—A Dominican Drama. The New York Times.

Waterman, R.A. (1947). Folk Music of Puerto Rico. Retrieved from https://www.loc.gov/folklife/LP/PuertoRicoAFS_L18.pdf